Travel Guide to Languedoc 2023

The Ultimate Guide to Discovering the Best of Languedoc for an Unforgettable Travel

Tania Clark

Copyright: Tania Clark 2023. Protected by copyright law. Except for brief quotations included in critical reviews and certain other noncommercial uses permitted by copyright law, no part of this publication may be reproduced, distributed, or transmitted in any form or by any means, including photocopying, recording, or other electronic or mechanical methods.

Travel Guide to Languedoc 2023

The Ultimate Guide to Discovering the best of Languedoc for an Unforgettable Travel

Tania Clark

Table of Content

Introduction
    Location and Geography
    Historical Summary
    Diversity of Culture
Travel Planning
    The Ideal Time to Visit
    Travel Necessities
    Visa and Entry Prerequisite
    Budgeting and Currency
How to Reach Languedoc
    Airports and Available Transportation
    Train Services
    Tips for Driving and Renting a Car
Languedoc's Accommodation Options
    Resorts and Hotels:
    Breakfast inns (Chambres d'Hôtes)
    Vacation Rentals
    Campgrounds:
    Selecting the Best Accommodation
Exploring Languedoc
    Major Towns and Cities
    Hidden Gems and Unusual Locations
    Local Food and Dining Options:
    Restaurant Experiences
Historical and Cultural Sites
    Medieval Fortresses and Castles

- Archaeological Sites and Roman Ruins
- Cathar Traditional Heritage
- Historical and Cultural Immersion

Festivals and Events: Celebrating Languedoc Life and Culture
- Festivals of Languedoc Wine
- Cultural and Musical Events
- Local Customs and Holidays
- How to Prepare for Festivals and Events

Arts and Crafts
- Local Artists and Workshops
- Traditional Souvenirs and Crafts:
- Investigating Arts and Crafts

Tips for Having a Memorable Languedoc Experience
- Communication and Language
- Health and Security:
- Sustainable Travel Methods
- Easily Getting Around Languedoc:

Plans for Day Trips: Discovering the Best of Languedoc
- Languedoc in One Week: A Comprehensive Tour
- Activities for the Whole Family: Special Moments for Everyone
- Culinary and Wine Adventures: Tasting the Flavors of Languedoc

Transportation Within Languedoc
- Public Transportation
- Routes for Cycling: Take the Scenic Routes
- River Cruising: A Relaxed Exploration
- Transportation Advice for a Smooth Journey

Shopping & Markets: Exploring the Treasures of Languedoc

    Markets & Bazaars Near You: Embracing Authenticity

    Unveiling Unique Finds at Specialty Stores

    Reasonable Shopping Advice

Language and Etiquette

    Basic French Phrases: Closing the Communication Gap

    Understanding Cultural Norms and Etiquette and Adopting Local Customs

Languedoc Navigation Made Simple

    Online Maps and Navigational Aids: Exploring with Care

    Conversion Charts: Using Measurements to Navigate

Your Journey with Confidence

Introduction

Languedoc, a mesmerizing area in the south of France, is a perfect fusion of the natural world, illustrious past, and active present. The topography, historical importance, and cultural variety of Languedoc are highlighted in this section's thorough overview.

Location and Geography

Beautiful Mediterranean beaches and untamed mountain ranges are both part of Languedoc's varied and attractive scenery. The Pyrenees Mountains to the south and the Cévennes Mountains to the north encircle this area, which is located along the Mediterranean coast. The diverse landscape makes a variety of outdoor activities possible, making Languedoc a paradise for adventurers and those who love the outdoors.

The region's climate, which is characterized by moderate winters and hot summers, is greatly influenced by its closeness to the Mediterranean Sea. The blooming vineyards and olive groves that dot the region are a result of the Mediterranean environment, adding to Languedoc's image as a wine-producing and culinary refuge.

Historical Summary

As varied and rich as its environment is the history of Languedoc. The area has seen the rise and fall of countless civilizations throughout antiquity, each of which left a permanent mark. The period of Roman control, when Languedoc thrived as a hub of commerce and culture, is one of the most notable historical chapters. Reminders of this historic history may be seen in the well-preserved Roman remains, such as the Pont du Gard aqueduct and the ancient city of Nîmes.

The advent of the Cathar movement ushered in a turbulent era throughout the Middle Ages. The Cathar heresy was centered in Languedoc, which led to confrontations like the Catholic Church's Albigensian Crusade. The fortified castles in the area referred to as "Cathar castles," built on cliffs and hilltops, bear witness to this period's heritage.

Languedoc has contributed significantly to the growth of the French wine industry in recent times. Visitors may learn about the long-standing wine-making customs that have been handed down through the years by visiting the region's vineyards, which have a colorful history.

Diversity of Culture

The cultural tapestry of Languedoc is fashioned from elements of numerous civilizations that have influenced its identity. The area has a special fusion of influences because of its closeness to Spain and its historical ties to North Africa. The architecture, gastronomy, and festivals of Languedoc all reflect this confluence of cultures.

Occitan, the language spoken there, is evidence of the distinctive cultural legacy of the area. Despite the fact that French is commonly spoken, Occitan is nevertheless revered by the people as a representation of their linguistic and cultural identity. By mingling with the local population and attending cultural acts, tourists may fully immerse themselves in the language.

Festivals in Languedoc provide a lively display of the region's cultural variety. These events, which range from vibrant carnivals to vivacious street parades, provide a window into the region's joie de vivre. For instance, the Feria de Nîmes is a well-known celebration that combines Spanish and

French traditions and includes bullfights, music, and dance.

The culinary scene in Languedoc reflects the region's blend of cultures and offers a mouthwatering selection of dishes that are influenced by both Mediterranean and continental flavors. Traditional Languedocian cuisine is based on locally obtained products, fresh fish, and fragrant herbs. Local markets, quaint bistros, and Michelin-starred restaurants all provide delicious food.

In conclusion, the intriguing area of Languedoc provides a well-balanced fusion of natural splendor, historical relevance, and cultural variety. The Languedoc region invites visitors to discover its varied terrain, illustrious history, and exciting present in order to create lifelong memories. Languedoc offers a rich and life-changing experience, whether one indulges in its gastronomic treats, explores its historic ruins, or takes part in its festivities.

Travel Planning

A trip to Languedoc has to be well planned in order to go smoothly and have fun. This section offers a thorough overview of trip preparation, including important topics like the ideal time to go, must-pack items, visa and entrance procedures, as well as currency and financial considerations.

The Ideal Time to Visit

Since the temperature in Languedoc changes throughout the year, it's important to decide when to go there depending on your preferences and interests. The area has hot summers and pleasant winters, with June to August traditionally being the busiest month for tourists. You may anticipate warm weather, crowded events, and a buzzing environment at this time. It's important to keep in mind that during certain months, popular sites and lodgings could be packed.

The shoulder seasons of spring (April to May) and autumn (September to October) provide great weather, fewer people, and the extra pleasure of blossoming flowers or changing foliage for those wanting a quiet experience. These are perhaps the best times of year for outdoor enthusiasts to go trekking and explore wineries.

With fewer tourists around, winter (November to February) might be a good time to go and enjoy the area's cultural attractions. Winter is a perfect time to enjoy the substantial food and regional wines of Languedoc, even if certain outdoor activities may be restricted by the weather.

Travel Necessities

Have the following travel necessities ready before starting your Languedoc adventure:

1. Travel insurance is necessary to give coverage in the event of unanticipated occurrences, such as medical crises, trip cancellations, or lost possessions.

2. **Health Precautions:** Before coming to Languedoc, find out whether any immunizations are necessary or advised. Carry a basic first aid kit and any essential prescriptions.

3. **Electrical Adapters:** France makes use of Type C common European outlets. Make sure you have

the right adapters on hand so you can charge your gadgets.

4. Having a rudimentary command of French words may improve your trip experience and interactions with locals, even if many people in tourist regions know English.

5. **Navigation Tools:** GPS navigation or map applications may be quite helpful for navigating the lovely villages, rolling countryside, and wineries of the Languedoc.

6. Languedoc provides a variety of outdoor activities and cultural discovery, so dress comfortably. Bring along sturdy walking shoes and layers of clothes for different climates.

Visa and Entry Prerequisite

The Schengen Agreement is a portion of France, which includes Languedoc. Most Western visitors, including those from the United States, Canada, and the European Union, do not need to have a visa in order to enter Languedoc for brief visits (often up to 90 days) for tourism. Before departing, you should confirm the precise admission requirements for your nation.

Make sure your passport is valid for at least six months after the day you want to travel. Maintain physical and digital copies of vital papers, including your passport, travel insurance, and emergency contact information.

Budgeting and Currency

The Euro (EUR) is France's official currency. In Languedoc, ATMs are commonly accessible, particularly in populated regions and popular tourist locations. In restaurants, hotels, and retail establishments, credit and debit cards are commonly accepted. To prevent any problems using your cards overseas, it's a good idea to let your bank know about your trip dates.

Budgeting for your vacation to Languedoc should take into account the following:

1. Accommodation choices vary from upscale resorts and boutique hotels to cost-effective hostels. Depending on the area and time of year, prices might change.

2. Dining: The gastronomic scene in Languedoc is diversified, with alternatives for every price range.

Enjoy a variety of eating options, from informal cafés to fine dining establishments.

3. Budgets for transportation costs, such as those for flights, trains, rental cars, and local transit within Languedoc.

4. Consider the price of admission fees to sights, guided tours, wine tastings, and other activities you want to partake in.

5. A budget should be set out for purchasing mementos, regional crafts, and items from markets and stores.

6. Having an emergency fund is a good idea in case unanticipated costs arise or your plans must be changed at the last minute.

In conclusion, careful preparation is essential for a fulfilling vacation to Languedoc. You may make the most of your trip to this alluring part of France by picking the ideal time to go, packing just what you need, being aware of visa requirements, and setting aside money for it.

How to Reach Languedoc

Your journey's first thrilling step is getting to Languedoc. This section offers a thorough overview of the many methods to get to this picturesque area, with details on airports, modes of transportation, rail services, vehicle rentals, and helpful driving advice.

Airports and Available Transportation

The area of Languedoc is well-served by air travel, with a number of airports acting as entry points. The main airports are as follows:

1. Montpellier-Méditerranée Airport (MPL): Convenient for passengers, this airport is located in Montpellier and provides both local and international flights.

2. Toulouse-Blagnac Airport (TLS) is a significant airport that acts as a hub for both local and international travel.

3. Nîmes-Alès-Camargue-Cévennes Airport (FNI): This airport, close to Nîmes, provides access to the

western region of Languedoc by domestic and seasonal flights.

4. Located close to Béziers, the **Béziers Cap d'Agde Airport (BZR)** offers service to several European cities, especially in the summer.

Travelers may choose from a variety of modes of transportation from the airport to get them to their intended location in Languedoc. Among these choices are:

- **Shuttle Services:** Numerous airports provide shuttle services for quick journeys to Languedoc's main cities and villages. It may be necessary to reserve certain services in advance.

- **Taxi Services:** Taxis are easily accessible at airports and provide a more individualized form of transportation to your lodging.

- **Public Transportation:** Some airports provide bus and tram connections to surrounding cities, making it affordable to get where you're going.

- **Rental Cars:** For those who prefer the freedom to explore Languedoc at their own speed, renting a vehicle is a popular option. Typically, rental vehicle companies are found around airports.

Train Services

Languedoc is well-connected to France's large rail network, making getting there by train both convenient and beautiful. Trains run by the French National Railway Company (SNCF) link the Languedoc region with important cities including Paris, Marseille, Lyon, and Toulouse. In Languedoc, important railroad stops include:

1. The central station in Montpellier-Saint-Roch acts as a significant rail node and provides access to a number of locations both inside Languedoc and outside.

2. Nîmes: The Nîmes railway station offers links to other significant cities as well as access to the western portion of the area.

3. This station, which is close to the medieval city of Carcassonne, provides connections to Toulouse and other adjacent cities.

As you ride through the French countryside by train, you may take in the beautiful scenery. It is a good idea to purchase rail tickets in advance, particularly during periods of high travel demand.

Tips for Driving and Renting a Car

Renting a vehicle gives you the opportunity to see the attractive cities, rural areas, and undiscovered attractions of Languedoc. The following advice should be kept in mind while hiring a car:

> 1. If your driver's license is not in French, make sure you also have a current international driving permit (IDP). Consult the rental company about the exact restrictions.

> 2. Navigation: Due to the complex road structure in Languedoc, GPS navigation equipment might be of great use. As an alternative, you might utilize a smartphone app for a map.

> 3. Become familiar with French traffic laws, such as those governing right-of-way, speed limits, and road signs.

4. Some French motorways have tolls that must be paid. Make sure you have enough cash or a credit card on you to pay for tolls or see if your rental vehicle has a toll payment system.

5. Parking: Parking spaces, both paid lots and on-street parking, are set aside in most municipalities. you avoid penalties, be sure you abide by parking restrictions.

6. Gas stations may be found in towns and along main thoroughfares. Remember that separate fueling stations may have varying hours, particularly in remote locations.

7. The majority of French drivers follow a stringent code of driving etiquette. Observe speed limits, use turn signals, and drive cautiously, especially on small roads.

8. Local Roads: Languedoc's picturesque pathways and side roads provide an opportunity to find lesser-known sights. Drive cautiously, however, since some country roads may be smaller and twisting.

9. Parking in Cities: Parking in urban cores may be difficult. Use park-and-ride facilities or look for authorized parking places.

In conclusion, there are a variety of ways to go to Languedoc, each with its own benefits. Planning beforehand and being aware of your transportation choices can help you have a smooth and enjoyable trip to this fascinating area of France, whether you decide to fly into the area's airports, board a picturesque train, or hire a vehicle to explore at your own speed.

Languedoc's Accommodation Options

Your Languedoc experience will be greatly impacted by your choice of lodging. This section explores the wide diversity of accommodation options available, including opulent hotels, quaint bed & breakfasts, one-of-a-kind vacation rentals, and rural campsites. any choice provides a different perspective on the allure of Languedoc, making it possible for any tourist to choose their perfect second home.

Resorts and Hotels:

There are several hotels and resorts in Languedoc that may accommodate guests with different tastes and inclinations. You may choose from options that provide lavish luxury or inviting comfort, depending on your preferences. Numerous of these facilities provide first-rate amenities, outstanding services, and stunning views of the surroundings. Consider the following categories of hotels and resorts:

    1. Discover lovely boutique hotels dispersed around Languedoc, each of which offers a

distinct and cozy ambiance. These places often include regional art, culture, and architecture while offering a distinctive experience.

2. Seaside Resorts: If the attraction of the Mediterranean appeals to you, think about booking a vacation at a beachfront hotel. Enjoy water sports, the breathtaking sea vistas, and the lively seaside atmosphere in the morning.

3. Countryside Retreats: For a tranquil getaway, choose a resort in the countryside that is tucked away among vineyards and undulating hills. Enjoy wine tastings, spa services, and fine cuisine while being in peace.

4. Historic Accommodations: Spend your time in a historic hotel or castle to really experience Languedoc's history. These homes combine luxurious contemporary amenities with a strong feeling of history.

Breakfast inns (Chambres d'Hôtes)

Bed & breakfasts, or "chambres d'hôtes," provide a genuine opportunity to experience the warm hospitality and local culture of Languedoc. These inviting accommodations, which are run by kind hosts, provide nice rooms and a prepared breakfast that often includes local fruit. You may meet locals while staying at a bed & breakfast, get tailored advice, and experience a cozy atmosphere. You can completely savor the allure of the area since many chambres d'hôtes are located in charming towns.

Vacation Rentals

For vacationers looking for a more autonomous and adaptable experience, vacation rentals are a popular option. Apartments, cottages, and villas are just a few of the rental choices available in the Languedoc region. You may have a private area, prepare your own meals, and live like a local by renting a holiday house. Vacation rentals provide you with a feeling of independence while immersing you in the local way of life, whether you're visiting a big metropolis or a peaceful town.

Campgrounds:

The campsites in Languedoc provide a unique method for outdoor explorers and nature lovers to take in the splendor of the area's natural surroundings. Camping areas may be found in picturesque areas including national parks, lakes, and the Mediterranean coast. Traditional tent camping, renting a camper van, or staying in a resort or cabin are all options. Camping not only offers a cost-effective choice, but also enables you to get close to nature and take part in outdoor activities like swimming, hiking, and stargazing.

Selecting the Best Accommodation

The following elements should be taken into account while choosing lodging in Languedoc:

> 1. Location: Choose whether you want to be in a busy city, out in the country, or close to the seashore.

> 2. Budget: Establish your spending limit and look for lodgings that go along with your financial strategy.

3. Consider your own priorities when choosing facilities, such as Wi-Fi, swimming pools, or on-site eating.

4. Local Experience: Opt for lodgings that let you engage with the local way of life and provide genuine experiences.

5. Depending on whether you're traveling alone, with a spouse, a family, or a group, choose accommodations that can accommodate your group in comfort.

6. Consider the activities you plan to partake in during your visit and choose lodgings that provide quick access to those activities.

In conclusion, Languedoc offers a wide range of lodging choices to accommodate the interests of every guest. While experiencing the beauty, history, and culture of this fascinating area, you'll discover the ideal location to lay your head, whether you're looking for luxury, intimacy, freedom, or absorption in nature.

Exploring Languedoc

The Languedoc region is a veritable treasure trove of stunning scenery, fascinating history, and delectable gastronomy. This section encourages you to set out on an educational tour of the region's main cities and villages, find off-the-beaten-path jewels, and enjoy the tastes of regional food.

Major Towns and Cities

1. Due to its thriving student population, Montpellier, a dynamic city, has a young spirit. Visit the beautiful Place de la Comédie, take in the ambiance of the bustling markets, and explore the old Old Town.

2. Toulouse: Toulouse, sometimes referred to as "La Ville Rose" (The Pink City), is a fusion of heritage and modernity. Explore the vibrant aerospace industry while admiring its gorgeous architecture, which includes the Basilica of Saint-Sernin.

3. Discover the well-preserved Roman amphitheater, the Maison Carrée temple, and the Pont du Gard aqueduct in Nîmes, where you can immerse yourself in Roman history. Enjoy the city's café scene and Provençal charm.

4. Step into a fantasy at Carcassonne, where a stronghold from the Middle Ages takes you back in time. Explore the majestic fortress, meander through cobblestone streets, and take in the expansive views from its walls.

5. Perpignan: Perpignan provides a distinctive cultural experience with a fusion of French and Catalan elements. Explore its markets, take in the Majorcan Kings' Palace, and savor Catalan cuisine.

Hidden Gems and Unusual Locations

1. Located in the hills, Minerve is a charming community renowned for its stunning setting and old-world charm. Discover its historic caverns, stroll through its medieval alleyways, and sample the local wines.

2. Collioure is a charming seaside town that charms with its vivid colors, artistic history, and beautiful beaches. Learn about its creative heritage, see the Royal Castle, and unwind by the Mediterranean.

3. Pezenas, a city rich in history and architecture, is home to an Old Town that has been exquisitely conserved. Discover the lively Saturday market, visit artisan studios, and discover the significance of Molière to the area.

4. Sète: A vibrant fishing port and center for the arts, Sète provides a unique fusion of the ocean, culture, and gastronomy. Take a stroll along its canals, see art museums, and eat delicious seafood.

5. Gorges de l'Hérault: The natural splendor of the Gorges de l'Hérault will appeal to nature lovers. Enjoy this beautiful river canyon for swimming, hiking, and kayaking.

Local Food and Dining Options:

The culinary scene in Languedoc is a feast for the senses, honoring the area's varied ingredients and illustrious traditions. You'll discover a variety of tastes to tempt your taste buds, from the fresh seafood by the shore to the substantial cuisine in the countryside.

> 1. White beans, sausages, and other meats are simmered in a rich and comforting stew known as cassoulet. It offers a genuine sense of the regional cooking of Languedoc.

> 2. Bouillabaisse: Enjoy bouillabaisse, a classic fish stew cooked with a variety of Mediterranean fish, shellfish, and flavorful herbs, along the seaside.

> 3. Oysters: Oysters from the Languedoc are prized for their delicate taste and freshness. They make a wonderful match with a glass of local Picpoul wine.

> 4. Enjoy a variety of handcrafted sausages, cured meats, and pâtés, often served with crusty bread and regional cheeses.

> 5. Cassoulet and Gardianne: Learn about many preparations of these rich beef stews, which are created with red wine and regional

herbs, and cassoulet, a slow-cooked bean and meat stew.

6. Languedoc produces a vast variety of wines, including reds, whites, and rosés, making it a wine lover's delight. Don't pass up the chance to tour nearby wineries and indulge in wine samples.

Restaurant Experiences

1. Visit local markets to really experience the gastronomic tradition of the Languedoc. Browse booths stocked with handcrafted goods, fresh fruit, cheeses, and meats.

2. Restaurants that emphasize locally produced, seasonal ingredients are known as "farm-to-table" establishments, where you may sample the greatest dishes from the Languedoc region.

3. The Michelin-starred restaurants in the area provide a fine dining experience, with talented chefs elevating regional ingredients to produce culinary wonders.

4. Picnics: Take advantage of unhurried picnics in gorgeous locations, such as by a riverbed, on a hill, or next to a vineyard. The ideal place to get picnic goods is at local markets.

In summary, discovering Languedoc is a multifaceted trip that reveals a tapestry of significant cities, undiscovered gems, and mouthwatering food. Every tourist can expect a unique and immersive experience thanks to Languedoc's charm, whether they want to explore the historic cities' fascinating histories, look for unusual locations, or sample the regional cuisine.

Historical and Cultural Sites

Languedoc's stunning Roman remains, medieval castles and the lasting effects of the Cathar movement are all evidence of the region's rich history and cultural heritage. The historical and cultural richness of Languedoc is explored in this part as you dig into its fascinating Cathar legacy, ancient Roman remains, and medieval castles and strongholds.

Medieval Fortresses and Castles

- 1. The well-known walled city of Carcassonne is a tribute to the defensive strength and architectural mastery of the Middle Ages. Visitors are immediately transported back to the Middle Ages by its imposing walls, towers, and drawbridges.

  2. Château de Peyrepertuse: This castle, perched high on a rocky slope, provides stunning panoramic views of the area. Its advantageous location and commanding

appearance highlight medieval military engineering.

3. Château de Quéribus: Quéribus, another of Languedoc's "Cathar castles," has a picturesque setting and provided a haven for Cathars during the Albigensian Crusade. Views of the Pyrenees may be seen while exploring its defensive walls.

4. Located within the walled city of Carcassonne, the Château Comtal provides insights into medieval life via its well-preserved chambers, walls, and exhibits.

5. Located in the Pyrenees, the **Château de Puilaurens** served as an essential fortress during the Cathar resistance. It is a must-see because of its majestic panoramas and commanding silhouette.

Archaeological Sites and Roman Ruins

1. Pont du Gard: The Pont du Gard aqueduct, a masterpiece of Roman engineering, crosses the Gardon River. Discover this UNESCO

World Heritage Site and be in awe of its meticulous construction.

2. The well-preserved Roman amphitheater at Nîmes, also known as the Arena of Nîmes, is a witness to the splendor of ancient entertainment. Learn about its history while marveling at its magnificent architecture.

3. Maison Carrée, Nîmes: This fascinating specimen of Corinthian architecture is a surprisingly well-preserved Roman temple. Investigate its inside to discover its historical importance.

4. Follow in the footsteps of early travelers as you traverse the Via Domitia, a former Roman route that linked Italy and Spain. Explore the remains of this ancient road.

5. Oppidum d'Ensérune: Investigate the archaeological site of Ensérune, a historic hilltop community that provides insights into the life of its Iron Age residents.

Cathar Traditional Heritage

1. The terrible history of the Cathars is inextricably tied to Montségur Castle, which is perched above a steep hilltop. Learn about its turbulent history and the tales of resistance it contains.

2. Château de Lastours: This collection of four castles provides a window into the Cathars' difficulties during the Albigensian Crusade. For expansive vistas, hike up to the castles.

3. Peyrepertuse and Quéribus Cathar Castles: These castles served as a final line of defense against the Crusaders and were a part of the Cathar resistance. Their commanding presence evokes an earlier time.

4. Cathar Trail: Set off on the Cathar Trail, a trek that passes through locations connected to the history, beliefs, and struggles of the Cathars.

5. Discover more about the Cathar movement and the Inquisition's effects at the

museum in Carcassonne, which has educational displays and historical relics.

Historical and Cultural Immersion

1. Participate in guided tours of these historic locations to learn more about their importance and the tales they contain. The stories told by local guides are amazing.

2. Visit medieval festivals and reenactments to experience the sights, sounds, and culture of the past. Medieval festivals and reenactments bring the history of the area to life.

3. Explore museums and interpretive centers that are devoted to the history of the area and that provide educational exhibitions, artifacts, and interactive exhibits.

In conclusion, Languedoc's historical and cultural attractions provide a fascinating trip through time that lets you see medieval castles, follow in the footsteps of prehistoric peoples, and learn more about the rich Cathar legacy. Each location has its own narrative to tell, opening a window into the past and enhancing your knowledge of Languedoc's rich and varied past.

Festivals and Events: Celebrating Languedoc Life and Culture

The whole year, the Languedoc area is alive with exciting festivals and activities. This section reveals the vibrant tapestry of festivals and events that give a distinctive dimension to the Languedoc experience, from celebrating the region's rich wine history to immersing oneself in the intriguing world of music and culture to participating in local customs.

Festivals of Languedoc Wine

1. **La Percée du Vin Jaune:** This event, which takes place in the Jura area, is a celebration of wine. However, many individuals all over the globe who are just getting into wine should attempt to keep in mind that if you are not a seasoned wine consumer, this area may not be the finest

spot to learn wine. The area of Languedoc itself has a number of magnificent wine festivals to honor its thriving vineyards. These festivities often include winemaker seminars, wine tastings of the best Languedoc vintages, and gastronomic experiences that match wine with regional specialties.

2. **Toques & Clochers:** This well-known event, which is held in Limoux, celebrates the union of wine and cuisine. It offers the chance to savor samples of great sparkling wines, discover gourmet food vendors, and take pleasure in the friendly environment.

3. Celebration of the tastes of Languedoc wines is held during the Fête des Vins in Narbonne. This exciting gathering provides tastings of a variety of regional wines, live entertainment, and chances to interact with winemakers.

4. Join in the celebration at Saint-Chinian's "White Night," where guests can have white wine tastings combined with scrumptious foods against the background of a quaint village environment.

5. The biggest organic wine expo in the world, Millésime Bio, is hosted in Montpellier and is a must-attend event for wine lovers. Browse a wide range of organic wine options and participate in debates about sustainable viticulture.

Cultural and Musical Events

1. The streets of Carcassonne come alive with a diverse fusion of music, dance, theater, and visual arts during the annual Festival de Carcassonne. Participate in outdoor concerts in historical locations to enjoy a variety of cultures.

2. Printemps des Comédiens is a theatrical festival held in Montpellier that features a diverse array of works, from traditional plays to cutting-edge modern pieces.

3. Jazz à Sète: At the Jazz à Sète event, music lovers may move to the jazz beats. Experience top-notch performances in a beautiful location with a view of the ocean.

4. Festival de Radio France et Montpellier: This famous music event draws performers and music enthusiasts from all over the globe. It features a broad range of classical and contemporary acts.

5. Experience the vibrant atmosphere of the Feria de Béziers, a traditional bullfighting and music event that honors the history and culture of the area.

Local Customs and Holidays

1. The vivid and centuries-old history of the Carnaval de Limoux is something to see. Participate in the vibrant parades, dance to the upbeat music, and enjoy the joyous atmosphere.

2. The nautical history of Sète is commemorated during the Fête de la Saint-Louis, which includes boat parades, water jousting contests, and energetic street acts.

3. Valras-Plage's Fête de la Mer is a time to honor the water and all that it has to offer.

Enjoy seafood feasts, activities with a marine theme, and a spectacular fireworks show.

4. Join the nationwide Fête de la Musique on the summer solstice, when streets and plazas come alive with live music performances featuring a range of genres and skills.

5. Celebrate the truffle during the Fête de la Truffe in Uzès to indulge in its scent and taste. Take part in truffle hunts, enjoy meals with truffle flavoring, and discover the nuances of this cherished delicacy.

How to Prepare for Festivals and Events

1. Advance Planning: To guarantee you can attend and make the required preparations, research the festival or event's dates and specifics in advance.

2. Book lodging in advance to ensure a pleasant stay, particularly during major events.

3. Tickets and reservations: Verify if they are necessary for certain festival events or performances.

4. To truly immerse oneself in the festival experience, get familiar with regional traditions and etiquette.

5. Planning your transportation to and from the event locations should take into account things like parking and available public transit.

To sum up, the festivals and events in Languedoc provide a fascinating look into the area's rich cultural legacy, from honoring the craft of winemaking to taking in live music performances and engaging in beloved regional customs. These events provide chances to meet people, get a sense of what makes Languedoc unique, and make enduring experiences that will be woven into the fabric of your Languedoc vacation forever.

Arts and Crafts

The artistic legacy of Languedoc is evidence of the area's strong cultural diversity and innovative spirit. This section digs into the world of Languedoc's arts and crafts, highlighting the commitment of local craftsmen and the charm of distinctive souvenirs that embody the spirit of the area. From talented artisans and workshops to traditional crafts that have lasted the test of time.

Local Artists and Workshops

1. Discover the craft of pottery and ceramics, as neighborhood artists turn clay into ornate items. Visit workshops to see artisans at work and peruse amazing goods that vary from colorful sculptures to useful kitchenware.

2. Glassblowing: Watch as talented artists sculpt molten glass into intricate shapes to discover the beauty of glassblowing. Visit studios that provide demonstrations and look through glass jewelry, vases, and decorations.

3. Textile Art: Drawing inspiration from local customs, Languedoc's textile artists create stunning textiles, tapestries, and clothing. Visit classes to learn about the world of textile art and to see weaving, dyeing, and stitching in action.

4. Discover the art of woodworking and carpentry, where craftspeople use age-old methods to create furniture, accessories, and musical instruments. Investigate workshops that display the exquisiteness of hand-carved wood.

5. Participate in pottery painting courses to express your creativity and create custom keepsakes by decorating clay objects with distinctive shapes and patterns.

Traditional Souvenirs and Crafts:

1. Admire the finely detailed Santons, which are hand-carved clay sculptures that represent scenes from traditional Provençal life. These endearing works of art make for lovely keepsakes that perfectly encapsulate Languedoc's past.

2. Explore the delicate realm of lace and embroidery, where skilled craftspeople make elaborate designs on cloth. Visit shops that sell handmade apparel, bedding, and accessories with amazing designs.

3. Explore the flavorful world of herbs and spices, and learn about the many Herbes de Provence mixes. Buy these aromatic blends as gifts to bring the scents of Languedoc to your home.

4. Take a bit of the Languedoc home with you by choosing hand-painted ceramics and dinnerware. These creative objects not only serve as useful objects but also as lovely mementos of your visit to the area.

5. Languedoc's world-famous wines and extra virgin olive oils are often beautifully packaged and make for considerate presents. To have a taste of Languedoc at home, choose from a variety of regional vintages and olive oil types.

Investigating Arts and Crafts

1. Visit regional markets where local craftsmen sell their goods, giving you the chance to speak with the creators and make unique purchases.

2. Workshops & Studios: Under the direction of experienced craftspeople, take part in practical workshops to learn about traditional crafts and make your own custom mementos.

3. Explore art galleries, boutiques, and craft stores that provide a carefully chosen selection of handcrafted items and artisanal goods.

4. Local Festivals: Many local festivals have craft fairs and exhibits, giving craftsmen a stage to display their creations and allowing guests to find one-of-a-kind treasures.

5. Cultural Centers: Look for museums and cultural institutions that emphasize the artistic legacy of the area and provide information on the development of traditional crafts.

In conclusion, the arts and crafts of Languedoc provide a way to engage with the region's creative heritage and harmonious fusion of history and modernity. The arts and crafts of the area provide an enthralling and genuine opportunity to connect with its cultural heritage, whether you're seeing the studios of regional craftsmen, taking part in seminars, or selecting souvenirs that capture the beauty of Languedoc.

Tips for Having a Memorable Languedoc Experience

To guarantee a comfortable and pleasurable vacation, traveling to Languedoc takes careful planning and a grasp of practical factors. This section offers crucial suggestions to improve your Languedoc experience, from overcoming language obstacles to putting health and safety first and adopting sustainable travel habits.

Communication and Language

1. Although French is the official language of Languedoc, you'll discover that many people there speak English, particularly in tourist regions. But making an effort to acquire a few fundamental French expressions might help you communicate more easily and demonstrate respect for the local way of life.

2. Utilize translation tools on your smartphone to help you overcome language barriers and streamline encounters, such as placing food orders, requesting directions, or striking up a discussion with locals.

3. Local dialects may enrich the endearing linguistic tapestry of Languedoc. Be aware that certain regions may have their own regional dialects or accents. Take advantage of the chance to get familiar with and grasp various language subtleties.

4. Politeness and Etiquette: In French society, being courteous and polite is valued highly. When engaging with locals, keep in mind to say "Bonjour" (good day) or "Bonsoir" (good evening), as well as "S'il vous plaît" (please) and "Merci" (thank you).

Health and Security:

1. Make sure you have comprehensive travel health insurance that covers medical costs, including emergency and repatriation before you go.

2. Medical Services: Become familiar with the locations of the hospitals, clinics, and other medical institutions in the region you're visiting. Keep a list of emergency phone numbers handy, including your embassy and the local ambulance service.

3. If you use prescription drugs, make sure you have enough on hand to last the length of your trip and carry a duplicate of your prescriptions. To bring pharmaceuticals into the nation, check the rules.

4. Pack sunscreen, sunglasses, a wide-brimmed hat, and lightweight clothes to shield yourself from the sun's rays since Languedoc has a warm, sunny environment.

5. Hydration: Keep yourself hydrated, particularly in the summer. Carry a reusable water bottle so you may avoid using unnecessary plastic and have access to fresh water.

6. Local Cuisine: Be aware of any food allergies or dietary restrictions while you indulge in the mouthwatering cuisine of Languedoc. Let restaurants know what you need, and think about carrying allergy cards in French to make sure your needs are understood.

7. Emergency services: Dial 112 for quick help in case of an emergency. The operators

can link you to the right services and they are multilingual.

Sustainable Travel Methods

1. Responsible consumption advises supporting neighborhood shops and independent creators by buying their products. Choose reusable goods to reduce the amount of single-use plastic trash, such as water bottles and shopping bags.

2. Rubbish Management: Respect the environment by recycling wherever practical and properly disposing of rubbish. Whenever possible, take part in events that promote wildlife preservation or beach cleaning.

3. Utilize trains, buses, and other forms of public transit to lessen traffic congestion and your carbon impact. The main towns and cities of Languedoc are connected by an effective public transportation system.

4. Walking and Cycling: By walking or cycling, you may explore cities, towns, and

the countryside while causing the least amount of environmental damage.

5. To protect the beautiful landscapes of Languedoc for future generations, abide by the trail's rules, and respect natural areas.

6. Be sensitive to cultural differences and respect regional traditions, customs, and historical landmarks. Observe set rules while visiting cultural and historical places, such as avoiding touching objects.

7. Choose lodgings that put an emphasis on sustainability principles, such as using energy-efficient equipment, reducing trash, and conserving resources.

Easily Getting Around Languedoc:

1. Learn about regional traditions, tipping norms, and business hours for local businesses and attractions. Local tourist information offices may provide insightful advice.

2. Currency and Payment: The Euro (€) is the accepted form of payment. Although

credit and debit cards are commonly used, it's always a good idea to have some cash on hand, particularly for smaller businesses.

3. The Languedoc region makes use of Europlug Type C and F electrical outlets. Make sure your gadgets are charged and have the proper adapters.

4. Consider the weather while choosing your gear, but also be ready for sudden changes in the weather. The intermittent nature of rain showers makes a portable umbrella or waterproof garment useful.

5. Local transit: To make taking public transit more convenient, think about buying passes or cards. If necessary, familiarize yourself with the bus and tram routes in your area.

6. Be mindful of the regular business hours in France, where certain stores and establishments could shut for a few hours in the afternoon. Make appropriate plans for your meals and activities.

To summarize, effective planning is essential for making the most of your Languedoc experience. You may completely immerse yourself in the beauty, history, and customs of this wonderful area while reducing possible problems by embracing linguistic subtlety, emphasizing health and safety, and adopting sustainable travel habits. An attentive attitude about your trips will improve your experience in Languedoc.

Plans for Day Trips: Discovering the Best of Languedoc

With its varied landscapes, extensive history, and lively culture, Languedoc entices visitors to go on a range of day trip activities. These painstakingly planned day trip itineraries provide something for everyone, guaranteeing that your stay in Languedoc is nothing short of amazing. Whether you have a week to immerse yourself in the area, are traveling with family, or are seeking gastronomic and wine experiences, they offer something for everyone.

Languedoc in One Week: A Comprehensive Tour

Montpellier is a city rich in culture and history.

> - Start your trip to the Languedoc at Montpellier, a lovely city. Explore the neighborhood art galleries and museums, enjoy the magnificent Place de la Comédie, and stroll through the ancient Old Town.

- Indulge in regional eateries' offerings of Mediterranean and other cuisines.

Day 2: Ancient Marvels in Nîmes and Pont du Gard

- Visit Nîmes to be amazed by the Maison Carrée temple and the perfectly restored Roman amphitheater.

- Keep on to the stunning Pont du Gard, a breathtaking Roman aqueduct. Take a leisurely lunch by the river and see this engineering masterpiece.

Day 3: Carcassonne - Magic of the Middle Ages

- Visit the historic fortress that resembles a fantasy, Carcassonne. Explore old walls, stroll through cobblestone streets, and take in the charming squares.

- Take a guided tour to learn about the city's fascinating history and enjoy the spectacular views from the castle walls.

Day 4: Hidden Gems in Minerve and the Canal du Midi

- Explore the alluring Minerve settlement, which is perched amid towering cliffs. Explore old caverns, stroll through historic neighborhoods, and visit nearby wineries.

- Travel to the UNESCO-listed Canal du Midi, where you may start a leisurely boat tour or bike ride along the picturesque canal.

Day 5: Coastal Charms in Pézenas and Sète

- Discover Pézenas, renowned for its Old Town that has been conserved and its connections to Molière. Visit artisanal studios and enjoy regional food.

- Travel to Sète, a bustling fishing town known for its canals, art galleries, and mouthwatering seafood. Enjoy a seafood feast and a leisurely walk along the waterfront.

Day 6: Coastal Beauty at Collioure and Banyuls-sur-Mer

- Visit Collioure, a beautiful seaside town renowned for its eye-catching hues and rich cultural history. Take a tour of the Royal Castle and relax by the Mediterranean.

- Continue on to the picturesque coastal town of Banyuls-sur-Mer, where you may indulge in wine tastings at nearby vineyards.

Day 7: Nature Retreat in the Cévennes National Park

- Visit the Cévennes National Park to round off your week. Immerse yourself in charming towns, deep woods, and green valleys.

- Climb Mont Aigoual for panoramic views to provide peace and natural beauty to the finish of your Languedoc excursion.

Activities for the Whole Family: Special Moments for Everyone

Day 1: Walled City Adventure in Aigues-Mortes

- Set off on a fun-filled family excursion in the walled and towered town of Aigues-Mortes. Discover the city's medieval past by strolling through its ancient streets and taking a tour with a guide.

- Enjoy ice cream with the family while enjoying the taste of Languedoc at a nearby café.

Day 2: Underwater Discovery at Aquarium Mare Nostrum, Montpellier

- Spend the day learning about the ocean at Montpellier's Aquarium Mare Nostrum. See a wide variety of marine life from the Mediterranean and beyond.

- Participate in interactive displays, feed fish, and get knowledge about initiatives to save the ocean.

Day 3: The Insect Adventure in Micropolis

- Travel to Micropolis, a unique park devoted to insects, on an intriguing tour. Explore themed gardens, interact with exotic insects, and take part in hands-on activities.

- With the help of engaging exhibitions and outdoor activities, introduce your family to the fascinating world of insects.

Day 4: Wildlife Encounter at Montpellier's Parc Zoologique de Lunaret

- For close contact with a wide variety of animals, including rhinos, giraffes, and big cats, go to Montpellier's Parc Zoologique de Lunaret.

- Explore the vast park, take part in educational activities, and have a family picnic in the great outdoors.

Day 5: Bamboo Wonderland (La Bambouseraie en Cévennes)

- Visit the fascinating botanical park La Bambouseraie in Cévennes, known for its bamboo forest and rare plant species.

- Walk through a landscape filled with tall bamboo shoots, cross suspension bridges, and savor the magical atmosphere.

Excitement at d'Agde Aqualand - Water Park on Day 6

- At Cap d'Agde Aqualand, an action-packed water park with pools, water slides, and aquatic activities for all ages, let the family's spirit of adventure loose.

- Enjoy a day of fun and relaxation by participating in water-based activities; great for families looking for adventure.

Roquefort Société Caves: A Cheese Exploration on Day Seven

- Travel to Roquefort to see the Société Caves and learn how the legendary Roquefort cheese is made.

- Enjoy tastings, guided tours, and the opportunity to see cheese being aged for an unforgettable and instructive culinary experience for the whole family.

Culinary and Wine Adventures: Tasting the Flavors of Languedoc

Day 1: Gastronomic Delights in Montpellier's Languedoc Market Tour

- Begin your gastronomic journey in Montpellier with a narrated market tour. Learn about regional cheeses, wines, and other gastronomic delicacies.

- Talk to merchants, discover local foods, and collect ingredients for forthcoming cooking adventures.

Day 2 of the Nîmes cooking class, "Mastering Provençal Cuisine"

- Attend a cooking lesson in Nîmes to learn the techniques for making true Provençal cuisine. Participate in hands-on culinary classes led by seasoned chefs.

- Savor the results of your effort over a delicious meal featuring your culinary innovations.

Day 3: Visit an Olive Grove and Partake in a Tasting - The Essence of Languedo

- Set off on a visit to an olive orchard where you may discover how olive oil is made. Take part in a tasting that shows the subtle differences between regional olive oils.

Day Four: Wine Tasting in the Minervois Vineyards

- Visit the famed wine-producing area of Minervois. Learn about winemaking, take guided tours of nearby vineyards, and enjoy samples of the finest Languedoc wines.

Day 5: Sète Seafood Feast - Coastal Delights

- Indulge in a seafood feast at Sète and appreciate the abundance of the shore. Enjoy delectable seafood specialties that have just been caught at a nearby restaurant that has a waterfront view.

Day 6: Roquefort-sur-Soulzon Fromage Tour - Cheese Sensation

- Set off for Roquefort-sur-Soulzon on a tour centered on cheese. Investigate cheese caves, discover the complex procedure for creating cheese, and have a delicious cheese tasting.

Day 7 will include a culinary workshop and a formal farewell dinner.

- In Pézenas, finish your culinary tour with a practical session. Create and enjoy fine cuisine that is inspired by the rich culinary tradition of the Languedoc.

- Toast your adventure with a fine dining goodbye meal, indulging in a sophisticated spread that captures the essence of Languedoc.

Finally, these painstakingly planned day trip itineraries provide a variety of activities that appeal to various tastes and interests. Languedoc encourages you to appreciate its beauty, culture, and cuisines whether you have one week to thoroughly explore the area, are looking for family-friendly activities that enthrall all ages or are keen to indulge in culinary and wine excursions. Your trip to the Languedoc will be filled with unforgettable experiences that perfectly reflect the spirit of this alluring area thanks to these well-planned itineraries.

Transportation Within Languedoc

A well-connected transportation network makes it simple to travel around the fascinating landscapes and lovely villages of Languedoc. Languedoc provides a variety of alternatives to make it easy and comfortable for you to explore the area, whether you prefer public transit, cycling along gorgeous roads, or taking leisurely river cruises.

Public Transportation

Languedoc has a robust and effective rail network, making it simple to go between major cities and villages. Regional and fast trains operated by the French National Railway Company (SNCF) link Languedoc to other regions of France, notably Paris. You can quickly go to places like Carcassonne, Béziers, and Perpignan from Montpellier and Nîmes.

- Buses and Trams: Public buses and trams are great ways to get through Languedoc's towns and cities. Modern tram networks link important locations and tourist sites in towns like Montpellier, Nîmes, and Béziers while providing easy transit. Buses are another dependable kind of transportation that connects urban and rural locations.

- Consider obtaining a transportation pass, such as the Occitanie Pass, which grants unrestricted access to local buses and trains throughout the Occitanie area. You may explore various areas of Languedoc at your own leisure with these flexible and affordable passes.

Routes for Cycling: Take the Scenic Routes

Languedoc has a network of bicycle lanes called véloroutes that wind through attractive landscapes, wineries, and historical buildings. Cycling along the canal banks along the flat and picturesque Canal du Midi is especially well-liked.

These "greenways" are exclusively for non-motorized traffic and are perfect for cyclists of all skill levels. They link towns and cities, provide safe and fun riding experiences, and highlight the area's natural beauty.

Cycling tourism is promoted by Languedoc, which provides tools and services including bike rentals, maintenance services, and lodging that is bicycle-friendly. It is simple to tour Languedoc on two wheels since so many municipalities have implemented bicycle-friendly policies.

River Cruising: A Relaxed Exploration

Canal cruises: The Canal du Midi, a UNESCO World Heritage site, provides a charming opportunity to see the scenery of Languedoc from a different angle. Many businesses provide canal cruises, letting you relax on board while floating by vineyards, old towns, and beautiful landscapes.

Consider taking a Rhône River cruise to see cities like Avignon, Arles, and Lyon if you're interested in learning more about the areas around the Languedoc. These cruises provide a variety of stunning riverside views and cultural activities.

The guided tours offered on river cruises may help you better comprehend the history and culture of the cities and landmarks you pass through. Even wine tastings, culinary excursions, and other regional features may be included in certain cruises.

Transportation Advice for a Smooth Journey

1. To make the most of your trip, research transportation timetables and choices in advance. Learn about the local transit websites and applications.

2. Timeliness: To avoid missing your journey, arrive at transit hubs (train stations, bus stops) early.

3. Purchasing tickets is possible at stations, online, or through mobile applications. If necessary, verify your ticket before boarding any trains or buses.

4. Although most major transportation hubs have English signs and workers, it's helpful to know essential words or terminology linked to transportation in French.

5. If you're thinking about cycling, find out about equipment requirements, rental possibilities, and suggested routes at the regional tourist information offices.

6. Reservations for river cruises should be made well in advance, particularly during periods of high tourist demand.

7. Carry water, food, a map, and a fully charged phone to keep yourself comfortable and connected while traveling.

In conclusion, getting about the Languedoc area is a smooth approach to seeing its varied landscapes and cultural treasures. The Languedoc region makes sure that your travel is as delightful and hassle-free as the sites themselves, offering convenient public transit, bicycle routes that highlight the region's natural beauty, and leisurely river cruises that provide interesting viewpoints.

Shopping & Markets: Exploring the Treasures of Languedoc

A lovely shopping experience in Languedoc mixes local markets with one-of-a-kind specialized shops. This section reveals the wide range of shopping options that enable you to take a bit of Languedoc's charm and character home with you, from lively local markets and bazaars to lovely boutiques and stores.

Markets & Bazaars Near You: Embracing Authenticity

The bustling Les Halles de Narbonne, a historic covered market where traders display fresh fruit, cheeses, charcuterie, and artisanal treats, is a must-see. As you browse the colorful kiosks and try the regional food, indulge in a sensory experience.

- Place aux Herbes in Uzès: This charming plaza is home to a bustling market. Take in the energetic mood there. Browse booths brimming with handicrafts, herbs, and seasonal produce, creating a rich tapestry of hues and fragrances.

- Les Halles Castellane, Montpellier: Les Halles Castellane is the center of Montpellier's gastronomic scene. With its wide variety of gourmet goods, fresh fish, meats, and mouthwatering pastries, this indoor market is a food lover's delight.

- Le Cours Saleya, Nice: Even if it's not quite in Languedoc, a trip to Nice's renowned flower and food market might be enjoyable. Enjoy the aromatic splendor of flower displays while perusing the kiosks selling handcrafted goods and Provençal delights.

- Carcassonne Market: This weekly market offers a mix of regional goods, including cheeses, olives, cured meats, and handcrafted crafts, all against the background of Carcassonne's ancient fortress. Enjoy the vibrant atmosphere as you stroll through this lovely market.

Unveiling Unique Finds at Specialty Stores

Languedoc has a long history of producing fine ceramics and pottery. Discover handmade items that vary from beautiful tiles and plates to complex vases and tableware by exploring nearby workshops and retailers.

Various lavender goods are available, including fragrant candles, soaps, sachets, and essential oils. Lavender is a well-known emblem of Provence. These aromatic mementos capture the spirit of the area.

The old villages of Languedoc sometimes have antique shops stocked to the gills with artifacts from bygone periods. Browse these shops to uncover one-of-a-kind furniture, antique fabrics, and lovely antiquities.

Buy regional wines and extra virgin olive oils from artisanal vineyards and olive mills to elevate your dining experiences. Choose unique cultivars that reflect the terroir of the Languedoc.

Cheddars, charcuterie, pâtés, and foie gras are just a few of the delectable local delicacies that you may get at fromageries and delicatessens. These delectable treats are perfect as presents or for treating yourself.

Explore artisanal shops that feature carefully created textiles, including woven and embroidered fabrics, as well as hand-stitched garments and accessories. These products showcase the skilled workmanship of the area.

Reasonable Shopping Advice

1. Both cash and credit cards are often accepted at markets and shops, but it's a good idea to have some cash on hand for smaller transactions and in more remote regions.

2. Open-Air Markets: To make the most of your shopping chances, learn when the local markets in the places you want to visit are held. Local markets are often hosted on specified days of the week.

3. Negotiating pricing is less prevalent in well-established stores, although it is acceptable at outdoor marketplaces and

bazaars. Negotiations should be conducted politely and respectfully.

4. Cultural Sensitivity: Be aware of regional traditions and manners while shopping, and always get permission before taking pictures of sellers or their wares.

5. Quality Over Quantity: Instead of accumulating a large number of trinkets, think about spending your money on a few emotive, high-quality mementos that capture the actual spirit of Languedoc.

6. Ask about shipping choices if you discover any bigger or more delicate products you want in order to make sure your purchases get to your house without incident.

Finally, shopping in Languedoc is a pleasurable experience that enables you to interact with regional culture, support local craftsmen, and bring home one-of-a-kind souvenirs from your trip. The retail environment in Languedoc provides a wide variety of treasures just waiting to be found, from lively markets bursting with fresh vegetables to specialist shops showing fine workmanship.

Language and Etiquette

Understanding the local language and following cultural norms and etiquette can improve your interactions and leave a great impression on the people you encounter while you travel across Languedoc. This part offers insightful explanations of fundamental French expressions and cultural customs that can enhance your encounter in this alluring locale.

Basic French Phrases: Closing the Communication Gap

Salutations and Courteous Expressions
- "Bonjour" (bohn-zhoor): Salutation for the day (used till dusk)
- "Bonsoir" (bohn-swahr): Good night (used from late afternoon to early evening)
"Merci" (mehr-see): I'm grateful
"S'il vous plaît" (seel voo pleh) means "Would you kindly"
"Excusez-moi" (ehk-skew-zay mwah) is French for "excuse me" or "I'm sorry."

Communication
"Parlez-vous anglais?" (par-lei vooz ahn-glay?) asks.

I speak French poorly. I say, "Je ne parle pas bien français" (zhuh nuh parl pah byan frahn-say).

- "Pouvez-vous m'aider?" pronounced "poo-veh voo meh-dey?"

Ordering Food and Beverages:
A table for two, if possible. - "Une table pour deux, s'il vous plaît" (ewn tabl poor duh, seel voo pleh).

The bill, please. - "Addition, please" (lah-dee-syon, seel voo pleh).

Numbers
- One, "Un" (uhn)
- "Deux" (obviously): Two
Three. - "Trois" (twah)
Four is "Quatre" (kahtr).
Five, "Cinq" (sank).

Directions
"Où est...?" (oo eh...?) means "Where is...?"
Right (ah drwat): "à droite"
- "à gauche" (ah gohsh): Left
"Tout droit" (to drwah) means forward

Understanding Cultural Norms and Etiquette and Adopting Local Customs

- Greetings & Politeness: The French put a high value on formal language and courteous gestures. Warm greetings with "Bonjour" are expected while entering a store, café, or other facility. Unless specifically requested to use their first name, always address them as "Monsieur" (sir) or "Madame" (madam), followed by their last name.

- When dining in Languedoc, it's traditional to have your hands out in plain sight above the table and to utilize utensils. Keep your hands on the table while speaking and wait for the host to start the meal before you start eating. As an expression of gratitude for the meal, finish everything on your plate.

- Punctuality: Being on time is seen as polite. Arriving on time shows that you have respect for other people, whether you are meeting someone for an appointment or participating in a group activity.

- Personal Space: Keep a suitable distance while conversing in order to respect personal space. Compared to some other cultures, French talks tend to include greater closeness but pay attention to signs of comfort.

- Dress Code: Despite Languedoc's informal environment, it is nevertheless important to dress correctly, particularly when visiting places of worship or upscale restaurants. Avoid dressing too casually in such situations.

- Gift-giving: It's considerate to bring a modest gift as a sign of thanks if you've been welcomed to someone's house. The recipient will appreciate receiving flowers, a bottle of wine, or a box of chocolates. Lilies should not be given since they are often given during funerals.

- Service fees are often included in the bill in Languedoc. However, giving a little extra tip is a way to express gratitude for excellent service. Leave a few euros on the table or round up the total.

- Discussing art, culture, gastronomy, and local issues will make you more social since the French value meaningful talks. When speaking, it's usual to make eye contact and utilize the proper titles and last names.

- Public Conduct: Languedoc places high importance on respect for others and a feeling of community. Be considerate of noise levels and refrain from speaking loudly in public, particularly during specified quiet hours.

- A kiss on each cheek is a typical way for friends and acquaintances to greet one another in Languedoc. Allow the other person to make the first move, and remember that handshakes are also a common way to welcome people.

- Religious Sites: When visiting churches or other places of worship, dress modestly and act with respect. Turn off the camera on your phone, and only take pictures when you have permission.

Your interactions and experiences in Languedoc will be greatly influenced by your command of the language and manners. By adhering to these cultural customs and picking up a few basic words, you'll be able to explore the area with ease and develop meaningful relationships with the people, which will help you get a better knowledge of the Languedoc's rich history and dynamic way of life.

Languedoc Navigation Made Simple

The appendix of this thorough Languedoc travel guide is a useful tool for helping you navigate the region's landscapes, comprehend measures, and find crucial contact information. You'll be equipped with the resources you need to maximize your Languedoc journey thanks to maps, conversion tables, and important contacts.

Online Maps and Navigational Aids: Exploring with Care

- Google Maps is a flexible tool that provides thorough maps, directions, and street views. Use it to map travel itineraries, identify sites of interest, and find local eateries, lodgings, and attractions.

- Offline Maps: Before setting off, you may want to download offline maps of Languedoc. This ensures you never get lost by giving you access to maps even when there is no internet connection.

- Websites of municipal tourism boards in Languedoc often include downloadable maps that emphasize the region's top sights, transit hubs, and suggested itineraries. These maps might be useful tools to complement your research.

Conversion Charts: Using Measurements to Navigate

The metric system is used for measures across France, including the Languedoc. Learn how to use metric units so you may more readily comprehend weights, temperatures, and distances you encounter while traveling.

- A kilometer is equal to 0.62 miles.
- One meter is equal to 3.28 feet.
- One degree Celsius (°C) is equal to eighteen degrees Fahrenheit (°F).
- One kg (kg) equals two pounds (lb)
1 liter (L) is equal to 0.26 gallons (gal).

Converting Currencies:
- 1 Euro (€) equals [Your currency] at the current exchange rate

Contact Details: Maintaining Contact

Emergency services include:
17 Police
18 Fire Department
- 15 medical emergencies

Your Journey with Confidence

An extensive toolset for traveling Languedoc with comfort and confidence is provided in the appendix. This section gives you the tools you need to make the most of your Languedoc experience, whether you're utilizing online maps to explore the area, referring to conversion tables to understand measures, or obtaining crucial contact information for emergencies or help. You'll be well-equipped to immerse yourself in the beauty, culture, and experiences that Languedoc has to offer if you have access to these resources. Happy travels!

We are left with an unforgettable tapestry of memories and experiences that have woven themselves into the very fabric of our souls as our adventure through the captivating landscapes, rich history, and lively culture of Languedoc comes to an end. With its timeless attractiveness and limitless beauty, Languedoc has welcomed us with open arms, asking us to discover its secret passageways, savor its delectable cuisine, and immerse ourselves in its enthralling tales.

The Languedoc region is a veritable gold mine of delights waiting to be found, from the ancient citadels that whisper tales of bygone ages to the sun-kissed vineyards that provide some of the world's most beautiful wines. We have traveled through busy marketplaces that are bursting with color and fragrance, and we have gazed in amazement at architectural wonders that are examples of human creativity.

We have strolled through beautiful nature reserves, felt the warmth of the Mediterranean beach under our feet, and taken leisurely cruises along tranquil canals that run through charming villages as we explored the many landscapes of Languedoc. From decadent cheeses to delicate wines that have been cultivated by the terroir from which they originate, we have experienced the products of the soil.

Beyond the obvious beauty and sensual joys, though, Languedoc's soul is what has really won our hearts. We will never forget the warm welcome we received from the inhabitants, their sincere grins, the joy we enjoyed over a leisurely supper with new acquaintances, and the connection we made with their folklore.

Let us take with us the lessons Languedoc has taught us as we say goodbye: lessons about history, cultural variety, and about the value of appreciating the little things in life. Wherever our travels may take us, let's keep in mind the cobblestone pathways that once resounded with the footfall of ancestors, and let's bring with us the flavor of those tastes and the warmth of their welcome.

May this book be your trusted travel companion as it leads you through the wonders and complexities of Languedoc. Whether you're a traveler looking for excitement, a family seeking priceless memories, or a connoisseur of art and food, Languedoc has welcomed you with open arms and left you with an imprint that will always serve as a reminder of the enchantment you experienced there.

The narrative of Languedoc is far from done as the last chapter of our trip draws to a conclusion. Its people will greet future tourists with the same warmth and kindness that has blessed our journeys, and its landscapes will continue to change. Additionally, its history will gain new chapters.

Carry Languedoc's spirit with you as you go forward as a reminder of the vastness of our world's splendor and the possibility for exploration, connection, and amazement around every bend. We appreciate you letting us be a part of your trip to Languedoc, and we wish you many exciting new experiences and priceless memories to come.

Good luck and may Languedoc's heart beat inside you always.

Printed in Great Britain
by Amazon